Fact Finders®

A Primary Source History of

U.S. INDEPENDENCE

by Krystyna Poray Goddu

Consultant: Matthew H. Crocker
Professor of History
Keene State College
Keene, New Hampshire

CAPSTONE PRESS
a capstone imprint

Fact Finders Books are published by Capstone Press,
1710 Roe Crest Drive, North Mankato, Minnesota 56003
www.capstonepub.com

Library of Congress Cataloging-in-Publication Data
Goddu, Krystyna Poray.
A primary source history of U.S. independence / by Krystyna Poray Goddu.
pages cm. — (Fact finders. Primary source history)
Summary: "Uses primary sources to tell the story of how the 13 colonies gained independence from
Great Britain"— Provided by publisher.
Includes bibliographical references and index.
ISBN 978-1-4914-1842-0 (library binding) — ISBN 978-1-4914-1846-8 (pbk.) —
ISBN 978-1-4914-1850-5 (ebook pdf)
1. United States—History—Colonial period, ca. 1600–1775—Juvenile literature. I. Title.
E188.G59 2015
973.2—dc23
                                                          2014032644

Editorial Credits
Jennifer Besel, editor; Kyle Grenz, designer; Wanda Winch, media researcher;
    Kathy McColley, production specialist

Photo Credits
Bridgeman Images: Peter Newark American Pictures/Private Collection/Johann Zoffany, 21, State
Historical Society of Wisconsin, Madison, USA, 5; Capstone, 25; Corbis: Blue Lantern Studio, 9;
Courtesy of the Massachusetts Historical Society, 14, 17, 19; CriaImages.com: Jay Robert Nash
Collection, cover; The Granger Collection, NYC, 7; Library of Congress: Prints and Photographs
Division, 1 (bottom), 11, 15, 20, 22, 27 (top), 28, 29, Rare Book Division Broadside Collection, cover
(inset); National Archives and Records Administration: www.ourdocuments.gov, 1 (t), 23; National
Parks Service: Colonial National Historical Park/Sidney E. King, 27 (b); North Wind Picture Archives,
6; SuperStock: Image Asset Management Ltd., 13; www.historicalimagebank.com, Painting by Don
Troiani, 16

Printed in Canada.
092014   008478FRS15

TABLE OF CONTENTS

A NOTE ABOUT PRIMARY SOURCES

Primary sources are newspaper articles, photographs, speeches, or other documents that were created during an event. They are great ways to see how people spoke and felt during that time. You'll find primary sources from events that led to U.S. independence throughout this book. Within the text, primary source quotations are colored *red* and set in italic type.

LAND OF THE FREE

"The Star Spangled Banner" declares the United States to be *"the land of the free."* But it took years of struggle and staggering losses to achieve that freedom.

In the 1600s and 1700s, many of the people who came to America were British subjects. They lived in British colonies and were officially under King George III's rule. For years the British government left the colonists alone, allowing them to make their own laws. While not independent, the people felt free.

By the middle of the 1700s, colonists found themselves involved in a war between France and Great Britain. The two sides battled over territories in North America. Colonists fought alongside British troops. American Indians joined with the French. This conflict became known as the French and Indian War (1754–1763).

When the war ended, France lost all its territory on mainland North America. But Great Britain worried that Indians would continue fighting. The British government refused to let colonists move to the new areas and left 10,000 troops in the colonies. This decision was the first of many that colonists would protest after the war.

△ A large number of American Indians joined the French during the French and Indian War. They hoped the French would help protect their lands.

Those protests would eventually build into a fight for *"Free and Independent States ... **Absolved** from all **Allegiance** to the British Crown,"* as the Declaration of Independence ultimately proclaimed.

absolve—to pardon something or free the person from blame
allegiance—loyal support for someone or something

HIGH COST OF VICTORY

Fighting the French and Indian War left Great Britain with an enormous debt. Because the victory benefited the colonists, **Parliament** believed colonists should help pay for it. In March 1765 lawmakers in Great Britain passed the Stamp Act to raise money. The act said that starting in November colonists had to buy British tax stamps for many paper products printed in America.

The colonists were shocked. They were used to electing representatives to colonial governments who collected any necessary taxes. Colonists did not elect any representatives to the British Parliament.

Colonists protested the Stamp Act by burning tax stamps in the street.

Parliament—a group of people who make laws and run the government in some countries

6

Connecticut governor Thomas Fitch wrote this pamphlet in 1764, protesting the new taxes.

▷

REASONS
WHY
The *BRITISH* COLONIES,
IN
AMERICA,
SHOULD NOT BE CHARGED WITH
INTERNAL TAXES,
BY AUTHORITY OF
PARLIAMENT;
HUMBLY OFFERED,
For CONSIDERATION,
In Behalf of the COLONY of
CONNECTICUT.

NEW-HAVEN:
Printed by B. MECOM. M,DCC,LXIV.

It suddenly became obvious that colonists had no voice in the government that ruled them. Connecticut's colonial governor, Thomas Fitch, wrote *"... the power lately exercised by Parliament of imposing taxes on the Colonies without their consent ... is inconsistent with the principles and spirit of the British constitution, and an infringement on the essential liberties of the colonies ..."*

But Parliament didn't understand why colonists were fighting the tax. British lawmaker Soame Jenyns found the American arguments filled with *"... **insolence** equal to their absurdity ..."*

insolence—insulting and outspoken behavior

PROTESTS BEGIN

The Stamp Act quickly divided colonists. British **Loyalists** argued that Parliament controlled them and could tax them. **Patriot** merchants refused to buy or sell British goods.

As tempers flared the Massachusetts legislature called for colonies to discuss the Stamp Act. In October 1765, 28 delegates from nine colonies met in New York at the Stamp Act Congress.

After much debate the delegates agreed that

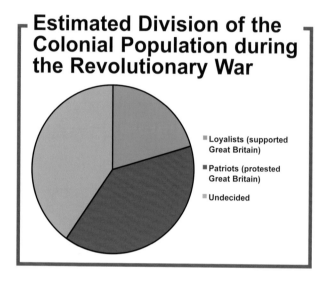

Estimated Division of the Colonial Population during the Revolutionary War

- Loyalists (supported Great Britain)
- Patriots (protested Great Britain)
- Undecided

"... His Majesty's subjects in these colonies owe the same allegiance to the crown of Great Britain that is owing from his subjects born within the realm ..."

However, the delegates also decided that because there were no representatives elected to Parliament from the colonies, Parliament could not tax them without their agreement.

"... [I]t is inseparably essential to the freedom of a people ... that no taxes be imposed on them, but with their own consent, given personally, or by their representatives ..."

Long after the Revolutionary War, artists created images showing the colonists rebelling against Britain. ▷

Leaders in Great Britain disagreed. They believed that since Britain owned the colonies, Parliament could do whatever it wanted there. George Grenville, Britain's former prime minister, claimed, *"Great Britain protects America, America is bound to yield obedience."*

When the Stamp Act went into effect in November, many colonists protested and refused to pay it. By March 1766 Parliament realized it couldn't collect the tax. It **repealed** the Stamp Act. The repeal was the first major victory for the colonists.

CRITICAL THINKING

Compare the quotations from Grenville and Jenyns with those from Fitch and the Stamp Act Congress. What do they reflect about how Parliament viewed the colonists and how the colonists viewed themselves?

Loyalist—a colonist who was loyal to Great Britain
Patriot—a person who sided with the colonies
repeal—to officially cancel something, such as a law

TROUBLE BREWS IN BOSTON

After the Stamp Act, Parliament was even more determined to show its power in America. The 1766 Declaratory Act announced Parliament's right *"to bind the colonies ... in all cases whatsoever."* Parliament could pass whatever laws it thought right. A year later it did just that with the Townshend Acts. This law put new taxes on glass, paint, oil, paper, and tea.

The Townshend Acts revived the colonists' anger. Again, Patriots **boycotted** British goods. Some Patriots even bullied those who ignored the boycott. Britain worried that it was losing control. Parliament sent more troops to the colonies to enforce the laws. The situation grew more tense every day.

The greatest friction was in Boston where 4,000 troops occupied the town. On the night of March 5, 1770, a rowdy group of colonists shouted insults at a soldier. Nasty words were followed by snowballs. A mob began to grow, swelling with violence. Captain Thomas Preston raced to the scene with more British soldiers. He later wrote about the scene. *"The mob still increased and were more outrageous, striking their clubs ... one against another, calling out, come on you rascals, you bloody backs, you lobster scoundrels, fire if you dare ..."*

boycott—to refuse to take part in something as a way of making a protest

The soldiers fired into the crowd. By the time the riot ended, five colonists were dead. Bostonian John Rowe wrote about the event in his diary. *"... A Quarrel between the soldiers & Inhabitants ... A Party of the 29th under the Command of Capt Preston fird on the People ... The Inhabitants are greatly enraged and not without Reason."*

▽ Patriot Paul Revere engraved this image of the events in Boston and released it to colonists on about March 28, 1770. His picture shows soldiers firing on quiet citizens.

CRITICAL THINKING

Compare Paul Revere's engraving of the Boston Massacre with Preston's account of the event. How do the two accounts differ? Why do you think they are different?

TEA TIME

After what became known as the Boston Massacre, the troops left Boston. A few years of relative peace followed. Because of colonists' resistance, Parliament repealed the Townshend Acts. The only tax that remained was a tax on tea.

But by 1773 the East India Tea Company was in serious financial trouble. The company paid thousands of **pounds** to the British government every year. If the company failed, the government would lose a great deal of money. To save the company, Parliament passed the Tea Act. This law allowed the company to sell tea without charging the tax.

Colonial tea merchants grew angry because they still had to pay tax on other teas. They believed Parliament was favoring the East India Tea Company. Citizens in Plymouth, Massachusetts, published editorials attacking the act as *"dangerous to the ... commerce of this country."* Further, they pledged *"to Aid & Support all our brethren in their opposition to this & Every Violation of our rights."*

Other Plymouth citizens feared the consequences of fighting against the act. They published their opinions, opposing any actions that might *"introduce anarchy, confusion, and disorder into the state."*

pound—the unit of money in the United Kingdom

In Boston three East India Tea Company ships docked in the harbor. On the night of December 16, 1773, a group of Patriots sneaked onto the ships. *"... [W]e cared no more for our lives than three straws, and determined to throw the tea overboard,"* recalled Patriot David Kennerson. In three hours they dumped 342 chests of tea into Boston Harbor.

Patriots were overjoyed at the act of rebellion. *"This is the grandest, Event, which has ever yet happened Since, the Controversy, with Britain, opened!"* wrote John Adams.

◁ Artist W. J. Palmer re-created the scene during the Boston Tea Party in this engraving from around 1850.

INTOLERABLE ACTS

King George and Parliament were furious about the "Boston Tea Party." Parliament closed Boston Harbor and issued harsh new laws. The British military commander in America became governor of Massachusetts. Colonists could no longer elect local officials. British troops returned and were allowed to live in private homes without the owners' permission. Parliament called these laws the Coercive Acts. Colonists called them the Intolerable Acts.

In September 1774, 55 delegates met in Philadelphia to try to settle the situation. Their purpose was to proclaim to Britain their unhappiness with the current laws. Their second, more difficult, job was to define their relationship with Britain. There was great disagreement. James Galloway of Pennsylvania argued that the colonies should make **amends** and *"... take such ground as shall firmly unite us under one system of [policy], and make us one people."*

amends—to make up for a mistake

△ In this reproduction of a drawing by H. A. Ogden, delegates leave Carpenter's Hall after a session of the First Continental Congress.

◁ Passed by Parliament on March 31, 1774, the Boston Port Bill closed Boston Harbor until colonists paid for the destroyed tea.

Benjamin Franklin, a diplomat from Pennsylvania, wrote to Galloway. Franklin was starting to think the colonies should be their own nation. *"... [W]hen I consider the extreme corruption ... in this old, rotten state, and the glorious public virtue so predominant in our rising country, I cannot but apprehend more mischief than benefit from a closer union."*

On October 14 the delegates of the First Continental Congress wrote to Parliament. They asked for a repeal of the laws they believed violated their rights. Then they shut off all trade with Britain.

FIGHTING BEGINS

The king and Parliament did not agree to the Congress' proposal. Many colonists were starting to believe the only solution was to become entirely free of Britain. They began preparing for war. **Militia** companies formed. Colonists stockpiled ammunition. Parliament declared the colonies in a state of rebellion.

People took sides with ever-growing passion. In March 1775 Patriot Patrick Henry declared, *"I know not what course others may take; but as for me, give me liberty, or give me death!"*

militia—a group of volunteer citizens who serve as soldiers in emergencies

A
NARRATIVE,
OF THE
EXCURSION and RAVAGES
OF THE
KING'S TROOPS
Under the Command of General GAGE,
On the nineteenth of APRIL, 1775.

TOGETHER WITH THE

DEPOSITIONS

Taken by ORDER of CONGRESS,
To support the Truth of it.

Published by AUTHORITY.

MASSACHUSETTS-BAY:

WORCESTER, Printed by ISAIAH THOMAS, by order
of the PROVINCIAL CONGRESS.

△ After the battles at Lexington and Concord, the Massachusetts Provincial Congress had Isaiah Thomas print this pamphlet as an official account of the battles.

◁ Minutemen, dressed in their regular clothes, stood up to the highly-trained British army during the Battle of Lexington.

Others agreed with Loyalist supporter Samuel Seabury. *"... [I]f I must be enslaved, let it be by a KING at least, and not by a parcel of upstart lawless Committee-men."*

On April 18, 1775, Patriots learned the British planned to march that night to Lexington, Massachusetts. They had two missions. The first was to arrest Patriot leaders John Hancock and Sam Adams. The second was to destroy a stockpile of ammunition in Concord.

Paul Revere and William Dawes alerted Hancock, Adams, and the militia. When the British arrived the next day, about 70 Minutemen were waiting.

And so the war began. Nobody knows who fired first. When the fighting was over, eight Minutemen were dead. The British had won the battle. But as they marched back to Boston, more colonial militia suddenly swarmed them. *"On our leaving Concord to return to Boston, they began to fire on us from behind the walls, ditches, trees ..."* reported a British leader. The colonists attacked fiercely, killing and wounding more than 100 British soldiers.

BATTLES WITH WEAPONS AND WORDS

As news of the battles spread, Patriots rushed to enlist in militias. Loyalists joined with the British troops.

On May 10, 1775, the Second Continental Congress met in Philadelphia to discuss how to handle the British military threat. The same day American rebels captured the British-held Fort Ticonderoga in New York. The capture surprised even the Continental Congress. Delegates voted to form the Continental army. They appointed George Washington to be the army's commander in chief.

Despite ongoing battles, many colonists still resisted war with Britain. On July 5, 1775, Congress tried again to peacefully resolve the problems. It sent King George the Olive Branch Petition. In it delegates wrote *"we not only ... desire the former harmony between her [Great Britain] and these Colonies may be restored, but that a concord may be established between them ..."*

King George refused to read it. He declared the colonists were *"misled by dangerous and ill designing men, and forgetting the allegiance which they owe to the power that has protected and supported them ..."* He vowed to convict anyone fighting against Great Britain of **treason**.

Printed in 1775 this map of the British battle plan was drawn by an officer at the Battle of Bunker Hill. Below the map appears a letter written by British General John Burgoyne to his nephew. The letter describes why the general felt *"it was absolutely necessary to become masters of these heights."*

▷

treason—the act of betraying one's country

A PLAN
of the
BATTLE,
on
BUNKERS HILL.
Fought on the 17.ᵗʰ of June 1775.
BY
an Officer on the Spot.

London, Printed for R. Sayer & J. Bennett N.ᵒ 53 in Fleet Street, as the Act directs 27 Nov.ʳ 1775.

The following Description of the Action near Boston, on the 17th of June, is taken from a Letter written by General Burgoyne to his Nephew Lord Stanley.

"Boston, June 25, 1775.

"BOSTON is a peninsula, joined to the main land only by a narrow neck, which on the first troubles Gen. Gage fortified; arms of the sea, and the harbour, surround the rest: on the other side one of these arms, to the North, is Charles-Town (or rather was, for it is now rubbish), and over it a large hill, which is also, like Boston, a peninsula; to the South of the town is a still larger scope of ground, containing three hills, joining also to the main by a tongue of land, and called Dorchester Neck: the heights as above described, both North and South, (in the soldier's phrase) command the town, that is, give an opportunity of erecting batteries above any that you can make against them, and consequently are much more advantageous. It was absolutely necessary we should make ourselves masters of these heights, and we proposed to begin with Dorchester, because from particular situation of batteries and shipping (too long to describe, and unintelligible to you if I did) it would evidently be effected without any considerable loss: every thing was accordingly disposed; my two colleagues and myself (who, by the bye, have never differed in one jot of military sentiment) had, in concert with Gen. Gage, formed the plan: Howe was to land the transports on one point, Clinton in the center, and I was to cannonade from the Causeway, or the Neck; each to take advantage of circumstances: the operations must have been very early; this was to have been executed on the 18th. On the 17th, at dawn of day, we found the enemy had pushed intrenchments with great diligence, during the night, on the heights of Charles-Town, and we evidently saw that every hour gave them fresh strength; it therefore became necessary to alter our plan, and attack on that side. Howe, as second in command, was detached with about 2000 men, and landed on the outward side of the peninsula, covered with shipping, without opposition; he was to advance from thence up the hill which

was over Charles-Town, where the strength of the enemy lay; he had under him Brigadier-General Pigot; Clinton and myself took our stand (for we had not any fixed post) in a large battery directly opposite to Charles-Town, and commanding it, and also reaching to the heights above it, and thereby facilitating Howe's attack. Howe's disposition was exceeding soldier-like; in my opinion it was perfect. As his first arm advanced up the hill, they met with a thousand impediments from strong fences, and were much exposed. They were also exceedingly hurt by musquetry from Charles-Town, though Clinton and I did not perceive it, till Howe sent us word by a boat, and desired us to set fire to the town, which was immediately done. We threw a parcel of shells, and the whole was instantly in flames. Our battery afterwards kept an incessant fire on the heights: it was seconded by a number of frigates, floating batteries, and one ship of the line.

"And now ensued one of the greatest scenes of war that can be conceived: if we look to the height, Howe's corps ascending the hill in the face of intrenchments, and in a very disadvantageous ground, was much engaged; and to the left the enemy pouring in fresh troops by thousands, over the land; and in the arm of the sea our ships and floating batteries cannonading them; strait before us a large and a noble town in one great blaze; the church steeples, being of timber, were great pyramids of fire above the rest; behind us the church steeples and heights of our own camp covered with spectators of the rest of our army which was not engaged; the hills round the country covered with spectators; the enemy all anxious suspence; the roar of cannon, mortars, and musquetry; the crash of churches, ships upon the stocks, and whole streets falling together in ruin, to fill the ear; the storm of the redoubts, with the objects above described, to fill the eye; and the reflection that perhaps a defeat was a final loss to the British empire in America, to fill the mind; made the whole a picture

and a complication of horror and importance beyond any thing that ever came to my lot to be witness to. I much lament Tom's* absence:—it was a sight for a young soldier that the longest service may not furnish again; and had he been with me he would likewise have been out of danger; for, except two cannon balls that went an hundred yards over our heads, we were not on any part of the direction of the enemy's shot. A moment of the day was critical: Howe's left were staggered; two battalions had been sent to reinforce them, but we perceived them on the beach seeming in embarrassment what way to march; Clinton, then next for business, took the part, without waiting for orders, to throw himself into a boat to head them; he arrived in time to be of service, the day ended with glory, and the success was most important, considering the ascendancy it gave the regular troops; but the loss was uncommon in officers for the numbers engaged.

"Howe was untouched, but his aid-de-camp Sherwin was killed; Jordan, a friend of Howe's, who came, engage du coeur, to see the campaign, (a ship-mate of ours on board the Cerberus, and who acted as aid-de-camp) is badly wounded. Pigot was unhurt, but he behaved like a hero. You will see the list of the loss. Poor Col. Abercrombie, who commanded the grenadiers, died yesterday of his wounds. Capt. Addison, our poor old friend, who arrived but the day before, and was to have dined with me on the day of the action, was also killed; his son was upon the field at the time. Major Mitchell is but very slightly hurt; he is out already; young Chetwynd's wound is also flight. Lord Percy's regiment has suffered the most, and behaved the best; his Lordship himself was not in the action:—Lord Roden behaved to a charm; his name is established for life."

* His nephew, the Hon. Tho. Stanley, Esq; (and brother to Lord Stanley), who is gone a volunteer to Boston, in his Majesty's service.

19

DECLARING INDEPENDENCE

Even before receiving King George's reply, Congress knew there was little hope for the Olive Branch Petition. The delegates continued to debate. Many were against independence, simply wanting fair representation in Parliament. When King George refused to read their petition, however, talk of independence grew louder.

In January 1776 Thomas Paine published his pamphlet *Common Sense*. *"I challenge the warmest advocate for reconciliation, to [show], a single advantage that this Continent can reap, by being connected with Great Britain ... We are already greater than the King wishes us to be, and will he not hereafter endeavor to make us less."*

the title page to Paine's ▷
Common Sense

COMMON SENSE;

ADDRESSED TO THE

INHABITANTS

OF

AMERICA,

On the following interesting

SUBJECTS.

I. Of the Origin and Design of Government in general, with concise Remarks on the English Constitution.

II. Of Monarchy and Hereditary Succession.

III. Thoughts on the present State of American Affairs.

IV. Of the present Ability of America, with some miscellaneous Reflections.

Man knows no Master save creating HEAVEN,
Or those whom choice and common good ordain.
THOMSON.

PHILADELPHIA;

Printed, and Sold, by R. BELL, in Third-Street.

MDCCLXXVI.

After the events of the past year, Paine's arguments made sense to many colonists. But others worried that creating a new government could be worse than being under the king. *"We have long flourished under our charter government,"* wrote clergyman William Smith. *"What may be the consequences of another form we cannot pronounce with certainty; but this we know, that it is a road we have not traveled and may be worse than it is described."*

CRITICAL THINKING

Compare Paine's argument for independence with Smith's argument to stay loyal to Great Britain. What action words does each person use to persuade others? How do these words support their opinions?

Throughout the first half of 1776, battles raged in the colonies. At the Continental Congress on June 7, Richard Henry Lee of Virginia asked delegates to vote on independence. He said, *"... these United Colonies are, and of right ought to be, free and independent States, that they are absolved from all allegiance to the British Crown, and that all political connection between them and the State of Great Britain is, and ought to be, totally dissolved."*

Seven delegates supported Lee's motion. Others worried *"that such a secession would weaken us."* Congress decided delegates should write to their colonies' legislatures for instructions. They would wait until July 1 to hold a vote.

While they waited a committee formed to write an explanation of why the colonists had the right to declare independence. Committee members chose Thomas Jefferson to write the first draft.

On July 2 Congress voted in favor of independence. On July 4, 1776, the Declaration of Independence was read. *"All men are created equal, that they are endowed by their Creator with certain inalienable rights, that among these are life, liberty and the pursuit of happiness. That to secure these rights, governments are instituted among men, deriving their just powers from the consent of the governed ..."*

By signing the Declaration, the delegates officially declared independence and became British traitors. If America lost the war, they could be hung for treason.

▷ the official signed copy of the Declaration of Independence

◁ This reproduction of a painting by Clyde Deland, that was printed in *Harper's Weekly* in 1897, shows Thomas Jefferson reading a rough draft of the Declaration to Benjamin Franklin.

After crowds in New York City heard the reading of the Declaration of Independence, they pulled down a statue of King George III. The statue was melted down, and the metal was molded into bullets for Patriot guns.

BATTLES OF THE REVOLUTION

Later that summer Washington's army was camped on Long Island, New York. The British forced the army off Long Island, into Manhattan, through New Jersey, and across the Delaware River.

The loss of New York made people wonder if Washington was the right person to lead the fight. Many soldiers left the army. Very little ammunition remained. The struggle seemed hopeless.

But Washington rallied. On a bitterly cold Christmas night, Patriots surprised the British by crossing the frozen Delaware River and defeating them in Trenton, New Jersey. Now people called Washington a hero.

An even greater turning point in the Revolution came with the American victory at Saratoga, New York, in October 1777. The British army lost more than three-quarters of its forces. After the battle British General Burgoyne described it in a letter to his nieces. He had been *"under perpetual fire ... sixteen almost sleepless nights without change of clothes, or other covering than the sky. I have been with my army within the jaws of famine ... my nearest friends killed round me ..."*

Major Battles of the Revolution

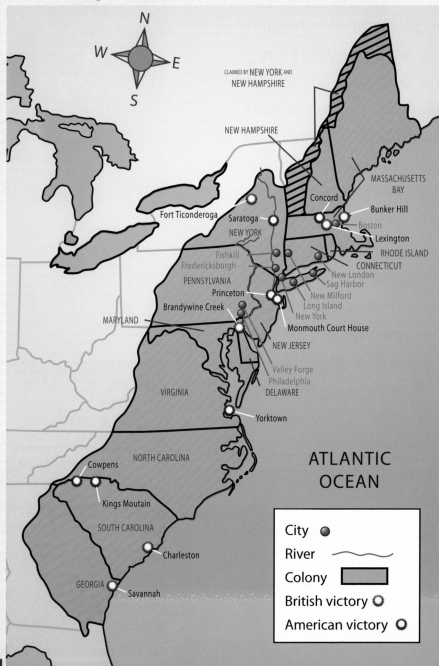

CLAIMED BY NEW YORK AND NEW HAMPSHIRE

NEW HAMPSHIRE

MASSACHUSETTS BAY

Concord

Bunker Hill

Fort Ticonderoga

Saratoga

Boston

NEW YORK

Lexington

RHODE ISLAND

Fishkill

CONNECTICUT

Fredericksburgh

New London

PENNSYLVANIA

Sag Harbor

Princeton

New Milford

Brandywine Creek

Long Island

MARYLAND

New York

Monmouth Court House

NEW JERSEY

Valley Forge

Philadelphia

VIRGINIA

DELAWARE

Yorktown

NORTH CAROLINA

ATLANTIC OCEAN

Cowpens

Kings Mountain

SOUTH CAROLINA

Charleston

GEORGIA

Savannah

City ●

River

Colony ▭

British victory ✷

American victory ✷

The Battle of Saratoga also convinced France that the colonists could win against Great Britain. Still angry about their loss in the French and Indian War, France agreed to help the colonies. Many historians believe the colonists might not have won the war if France had not sent help.

WINS AND LOSSES

After the victory at Saratoga, Washington settled his army for the winter in Valley Forge, Pennsylvania. It was a terrible winter. Soldiers built huts from mud and logs or lived in tents. They didn't have enough food or clothing. Some were forced to go barefoot, and bloody footprints covered the snow. More than 2,000 soldiers died.

Washington wrote to his friend and fellow soldier George Clinton for help. *"For some days past, there has been little less, than a famine in camp. A part of the army has been a week, without any kind of flesh [meat], and the rest for three or four days ... if you can devise any means to procure a quantity of cattle ... for the use of this army ... you will render a most essential service to the common cause."*

Despite the horrible conditions, the soldiers trained through the winter. They emerged a stronger army. Over the next few years they fought numerous battles. In some they claimed victory. In others the British defeated them.

In October 1781 Washington secretly brought his troops to Yorktown, Virginia. The British had seized the city. But the Patriots trapped and tricked them. They arrived in the dark of night and on October 9 began firing. After several days, the British were forced to surrender.

The war was not over, but the British army was much weaker. Following this defeat, Parliament began to discuss possible terms of a peace treaty. It grew clear to both sides that the Revolution was ending—and the Americans had won.

FREEDOM

Throughout the war the Continental Congress debated how to form a new government. On November 15, 1777, Congress adopted the Articles of Confederation. Colonies agreed to follow these laws and become one nation. Article One named this new country. *"The Style of this confederacy shall be the United States of America."*

When news came of the defeat at Yorktown, King George wanted to continue fighting. *"... [I]t is all over!"* the British prime minister declared. On November 30, 1782, Great Britain signed a preliminary agreement recognizing the independent United States.

The official peace treaty was signed September 3, 1783. American and British representatives met in Paris, France. The Treaty of Paris officially declared, *"His Britannic Majesty acknowledges the said United States ... to be free sovereign and Independent States."*

This reproduction of a painting by C. Seller depicts the signing of the preliminary treaty in 1782.

After nearly 20 years of debate and struggle, Americans had formed a new country. The colonists did more, however, than win freedom for themselves. The nation they fought to form became one of the world's most powerful leaders. The effects of the American Revolution reached far beyond America and changed the world.

In 1789 delegates met to discuss the Articles of Confederation. They realized those rules weren't as powerful as they needed to be. So they again debated and developed the U.S. Constitution we know today.

the first page of the Articles of Confederation

SELECTED BIBLIOGRAPHY

Adams, John. "To James Warren." December 17, 1773. The Adams Papers. Online by the Massachusetts Historical Society. www.masshist.org/publications/apde/portia.php?id=PJA02d001

"Articles of Confederation and Perpetual Union." November 15, 1777. Online by The Library of Congress. www.loc.gov/rr/program/bib/ourdocs/articles.html

"Declaration of Independence." July 4, 1776. Online by the National Archives and Records Administration. www.archives.gov/exhibits/charters/declaration.html

George III. "Proclamation of Rebellion." August 23, 1775. Online by Britannia's British History Department. www.britannia.com/history/docs/procreb.html

Henry, Patrick. "Liberty or Death." March 23, 1775. Online by the Patrick Henry Center for Individual Liberty. www.patrickhenrycenter.com/Speeches.aspx#LIBERTY

Johnson, William Samuel. "Declaration of Rights and Grievance," October 19, 1765. Manuscript. Manuscript Division, Library of Congress. www.loc.gov/exhibits/creating-the-united-states/revolution-of-the-mind.html#obj12

Preston, Captain Thomas. "Account of the Boston Massacre." Online by the Boston Massacre Historical Society. www.bostonmassacre.net/trial/acct-preston1.htm

Rowe, John. "John Rowe Diaries." Online by the Massachusetts Historical Society. www.masshist.org/revolution/resources/rowes.php#diaries

Seabury, Reverend Samuel. "Free Thoughts, on the Proceedings of the Continental Congress, Held at Philadelphia Sept. 5, 1774." Online by Project Canterbury. anglicanhistory.org/usa/seabury/farmer/01.html

GLOSSARY

absolve (ab-ZOLV)—to pardon something or free the person from blame

allegiance (uh-LEE-junss)—loyal support for someone or something

amends (uh-MENDS)—to make up for a mistake

boycott (BOY-kot)—to refuse to take part in something as a way of making a protest

insolence (IN-suh-luns)—insulting and outspoken behavior

Loyalist (LOI-uh-list)—a colonist who was loyal to Great Britain during the Revolutionary War

militia (muh-LISH-uh)—a group of volunteer citizens who serve as soldiers in emergencies

Parliament (PAR-luh-muhnt)—a group of people who make laws and run the government in some countries

Patriot (PAY-tree-uht)—a person who sided with the colonies during the Revolutionary War

pound (POUND)—the unit of money in the United Kingdom

repeal (ri-PEEL)—to officially cancel something, such as a law

treason (TREE-zuhn)—the act of betraying one's country

INTERNET SITES

FactHound offers a safe, fun way to find Internet sites related to this book. All of the sites on FactHound have been researched by our staff.

Here's all you do:

Visit *www.facthound.com*

Type in this code: 9781491418420

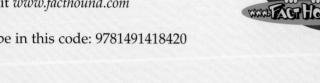

Check out projects, games and lots more at
www.capstonekids.com

INDEX